# *The*
# *PILGRIM STORY*

**BEING LARGELY A COMPILATION FROM THE DOCUMENTS OF GOVERNOR BRADFORD AND GOVERNOR WINSLOW, SEVERALLY AND COLLABORATION; TOGETHER WITH A OF MAYFLOWER PASSENGERS.**

**Compiled and written by**

**WILLIAM FRANKLIN ATWOOD**

**ILLUSTRATED BY LEO SCHREIBER**

**Published by THE MEMORIAL PRESS, Plymouth, Mass.**

Copyright 1940
By
PAUL W. BITTINGER
Plymouth, Mass.

Second Edition
October, 1947

Third Edition
June, 1950

Fourth Edition
June, 1952

Fifth Edition
April, 1955

Sixth Edition (revised)
April, 1958

Seventh Edition
January, 1963

Eighth Edition
January, 1966

Ninth Edition
April, 1968

Tenth Edition
May 1971

Printed and Bound by The Memorial Press, Plymouth, Mass.

# CONTENTS

---

## Index to Illustrations

NOTE—Many well-known pictures of the Pilgrims have grossly misinterpreted their true spirit. A "Signing of the Compact" or a "Departure from Delfthaven," for example, that employs the sentimental piety, the eyes and arms raised to heaven, of Italian Baroque art, (that Jesuitical, most Catholic art), fails to reflect the real spirit of the Protestant Pilgrims. The use of the gracefully reclining and swooning figures of Italianate renaissance art is likewise inappropriate.

Reacting sharply from this, the illustrations in the book portray in the modern spirit both the activities of the Pilgrims and their settings with strict realism.

Unsparing effort in consulting authorities, old documents, prints, and actual scenes was expended to secure convincing authenticity.

## PREFACE

No phase of early American history presents a finer example of faith, fortitude and determination of purpose than the story of that little band of devout souls who landed at Plymouth in the winter of 1620 and to whom we refer as the Pilgrims.

In the following limited pages the writer attempts to present something of the conditions obtaining in England prior to the Departure, also something of the struggles, privations, courage and forbearance during the first years of the settlement at Plymouth.

In so doing dependence is placed particularly upon the contemporaneous writings of Bradford and Winslow, both members of the Mayflower party.

With the vast bibliography relating to the Pilgrim history, together with the requirements of brevity, it is indeed fortunate that we are able to look to those who played such an important part in this historic episode and who were thoughtful enough to leave a record for posterity.

It is difficult to epitomize a story so broad and sweeping in its ramifications, its religious and material aspects and its touch of romanticism. Consequently it is intended to include only such events as may prove of interest and value to the reader as adduced from the recognized authorities.

These authorities as before indicated are:

Bradford, William: History of Plimouth Plantation. (Printed from the original manuscript in 1898 under the supervision of the Secretary of the Commonwealth of Massachusetts.)

Young, Alexander: Chronicles of the Pilgrim Fathers. (1880.) Including Mourt's Relation (London 1622) by William Bradford and Edward Winslow in collaboration; Good News from England, Winslow's Journal of 1622-23 (London 1624); Winslow's Relation and Winslow's Brief Narrative.

Hazard, Ebenezer; Hazard's Historical Collections, Vol. 1. Including Old Colony and Plymouth Records, Philadelphia (1812).

Note:—With regard to the original manuscript of Bradford's History of Plymouth Plantation, it may be stated that it was first obtained by Thomas Prince, the historian, from Judge Sewall, to whom it was "lent but only lent" by Major John Bradford of Kingston, son of Major William Bradford, formerly Deputy Governor of the Plymouth Colony, and grandson of Governor William Bradford.

This precious document which seems to have passed through several hands, finally found refuge, together with Prince's library, in the tower of the Old South Church in Boston, whence it later disappeared.

In 1856 it was found in the library of the Lord Bishop of London, at Fulham Palace. A transcript was made and it was printed in Boston the same year, under the auspices of the Massachusetts Historical Society.

In 1897 the original manuscript was brought to this country by the Hon. Thomas F. Bayard, our Ambassador to England at the time, to whom it had been delivered by the Rt. Rev. Mandell Creighton, Lord Bishop of London. Much credit is due to the late Senator George F. Hoar of Massachusetts, to the former Bishop of London, Dr. Temple, who later became the Archbishop of Canterbury, and the aforementioned Ambassador Bayard, who were all in accord as to the right and justice of the transfer.

This historic document now reposes in the state library in the State House in Boston, priceless in both historic and sentimental value.

W. F. A.

# FOREWORD

## Expansion on Cape Cod

The early settlements on Cape Cod all came about under the aegis of the parent colony in Plymouth. Several times in Pilgrim chronicles we read how Captain Myles Standish was sent to Sandwich, Barnstable and Yarmouth on tours of inspection and to supervise the division of lands purchased for little or nothing by the newcomers from the remnants of an Indian population decimated years before by disease.

Direct Pilgrim influence on the religious life, the administration and the courts of the Cape settlements continued from the earliest beginnings at Sandwich in 1637, with steadily dimishing strength, until the election of Thomas Prence of Eastham as Governor of Plymouth Colony in 1657. Meanwhile the parents settlement itself was coming under the domination of the Massachusetts Bay Colony and its Puritan hierarchs. The Plymouth connection finally lapsed, for all practical purposes, in 1685, when Plymouth Colony was divided up into Plymouth, Barnstable and Bristol Counties.

First Cape settlement was in 1637, when a band of Puritan families from Saugus and Lynn on the North Shore got permission from the Pilgrim Fathers to migrate to the precincts of the Plymouth Colony, of which the Cape was a part. Some Pilgrim families from Duxbury and Plymouth came along with these first settlers to carve out homesteads in the Sandwich area.

Next towns to be settled were Yarmouth and Barnstable, in 1639, an earlier attempt to populate the Mattacheesett section of what is now Barnstable having failed.

Yarmouth was a direct offshoot of Pilgrim Plymouth, and prominent among its settlers was Giles Hopkins, son of Stephen Hopkins, who came over with his father on the Mayflower.

Barnstable, at its inception, was dominated by the personality of the Rev. John Lothrop, a very strongminded man of dissident Pilgrim persuasion who, together with fifty of his parishioners, had once served two years in jail in England for religious schism. For a time the spirit of controversy continued in the new Cape Colony, fanned by the radical views of Marmaduke Matthews, a firebrand Welshman. But by the time Captain Myles Standish and two companions came down from Plymouth in 1643 to divide up the salt hay marshes, cleared farmlands and woods of Barnstable into legally recorded homesteads, the colony had settled down and become absorbed with more workaday matters.

Last of the very early Cape Cod towns to be settled was Eastham in 1644, by a party led by the Rev. John Mayo, bearer of another of the names later to become famous on the Cape in its great mercantilist period.

Falmouth, in 1686, fissioned off quite directly from Plymouth, and was incorporated in 1686, originally under the name of Succonesset. Harwich officially came into being in 1694, as an offshoot from Barnstable, and very much later, in 1803, gave rise to Brewster. Dennis, meanwhile, had fissioned from Yarmouth in 1794. But by this time Pilgrim origins and influence were but the dimmest of memories.

Also influential on the early Cape, after the middle 1650's, were the Quakers, at first persecuted, but eventually accepted as a manifestly superior kind of people. They, too, quickly merged during the following century into the Cape Cod way of life, and became indistinguishable from families of Pilgrim or Puritan origin.

## CHAPTER I — Scrooby: Persecution

The Pilgrim story may well begin from the period of the Reformation or the ascendency of the Protestant Church in England. Previous to 1600 much friction had existed between the Crown and the Papacy in matters ecclesiastical and civil. The process of reform however had been crystalizing during the reign of Queen Elizabeth. This came to culmination in the establishment of the English Church (known as the Church of England) as the official or state church of which the King was to be the temporal head with the Archbishop of Canterbury, the spiritual head or primate.

But still there was friction. It was like a house divided against itself. There were those who could not conscientiously subscribe to the laws and rituals laid down by the established church. They were dissenters or non-conformists and are best described by Bradford as follows: "The one side labored to have the right worship of God and discipline of Christ established in the Church, according to the simplicity of the gospel, without the mixture of men's inventions, and to have and be ruled by the laws of God's word, dispensed in those offices and by those officers of Pastors, Teachers and Elders, etc., according to the Scriptures."

"The other party endeavored to have episcopal dignity (after the popish manner) with their large power and jurisdiction still retained."

This strained and anomalous situation led to the founding of the Separatist Church in 1602 in the Old Hall in Gainsborough, with John Smyth as pastor.

Smyth was highly esteemed by the non-conformist group. He was a graduate of Cambridge, "an eminent man in his time," and his pastorate at Gainsborough extended from 1602 until 1606 when he was forced to retire.

The Scrooby fraternity, an off-shoot from Gainsborough, was presided over by Richard Clyfton as first pastor. Prominent among the non-conformists at Scrooby were William Brewster, born in Scrooby in 1560, William Bradford, born in Austerfield, a village three miles distant, in 1588, and John Robinson, born in Lincolnshire about 1576. Robinson received orders from the Church of England, was suspended for non-conformity and later joined the Congregation at Scrooby where he was made pastor.

This triumvirate became the ruling spirits of the Scrooby community, Brewster became the Elder of the Church and later the religious leader of the Plymouth settlement, of which Bradford became Governor. Robinson, to whom both looked for inspiration and guidance, was destined by circumstances to remain in Holland where he had later been forced to take refuge.

These independent thinkers who firmly asserted their right to worship according to their belief, were brought into constant conflict with the constituted authorities of the Church of England. As Bradford says: "This contention was so great, as neither the honour of God, the common persecution, nor the mediation of Mr. Calvin and other worthies of the Lord in those places, could prevail with those thus episcopally minded, but they proceeded by all means to disturb the peace of this poor persecuted church,

Note: In the subject matter in quotations, the spelling of some words has been changed to the modern form without otherwise affecting the text.

GREAT NORTH
ROAD
Saracens Head Inn
Moat
Ryton River
Only Part Now Remaining
BREWSTER MANOR
First Meeting Place of the Pilgrims
SCROOBY IN 1620

even so far as to charge (very unjustly and ungodly, yet prelate like) some of their chief opposers, with rebellion and high treason . . . " And then regarding their treatment he says: "They could not long continue in any peaceable condition but were hunted and persecuted on every side."

From 1603 when King James I succeeded Elizabeth who had reigned as Queen during the preceding forty-five years, conditions grew increasingly worse until as Bradford continues:

"Seeing themselves thus molested and that there was no hope of their continuance there, they resolved to go into the Low Countries, where they heard was freedom of religion for all men; as also how sundry from London, and other parts of the land had been exiled and persecuted for the same cause, and were gone thither and lived at Amsterdam and in other places of the land. So after they had continued together about a year, and kept their meetings every sabbath, in one place or other, exercising the worship of God amongst themselves, notwithstanding all the diligence and malice of their adversaries, they seeing they could no longer continue in that condition, they resolved to get over into Holland as they could which was in the year 1607-1608."

## CHAPTER II — Escape: Holland

*The Migration to Holland* was not accomplished without its set-backs and misgivings. In the first place it was unlawful under an old statute which made emigrating without authority a penal crime. They were several times intercepted in their attempt to depart from English soil. But they were determined in purpose and brave in heart.

"Being thus constrained to leave their native country, their lands and livings, and all their friends and familiar acquaintance, it was much, and thought marvellous by many. But to go into a country they knew not, but by hearsay, where they must learn a new language, and get their livings they knew not how, it being a dear place, and subject to the miseries of war,* it was by many thought an adventure almost desperate, a case intolerable, and a misery worse than death; especially seeing they were not acquainted with trades nor traffic, (by which the country doth subsist) but had only been used to a plain country life and the innocent trade of husbandry. But these things

*The religious wars involving England, Holland and Spain.

did not dismay them, (although they did sometimes trouble them,) for their desires were set on the ways of God, and to enjoy his ordinances. But they rested on his providence, and knew whom they had believed. Yet this was not all. For although they could not stay, yet were they not suffered to go; but the ports and havens were shut against them, so as they were fain to seek secret means of conveyance, and to fee the mariners, and give extraordinary rates for their passages. And yet were they oftentimes betrayed, many of them, and both they and their goods intercepted and surprised, and thereby put to great trouble and charge; of which I will give an instance or two, and omit the rest."

"There was a great company of them purposed to get passage at Boston, in Lincolnshire; and for that end had hired a ship wholly to themselves, and made agreement with the master to be ready at a certain day, and take them and their goods in, at a convenient place, where they accordingly would all attend in readiness. So after long waiting and large expenses, though he kept not the day with them, yet he came at length, and took them in, in the night. And when he had them and their goods aboard, he betrayed them, having beforehand complotted with the searchers and other officers so to do; who took them and put them into open boats, and there rifled and ransacked them, searching them to their shirts for money, yae, even the women, further than became modesty; and then carried them back into the town, and made them a spectacle and wonderment to the multitude, which came flocking on all sides to behold them. Being thus by the catchpole officers riffled and stripped of their money, books and much other goods, they were presented to the magistrates, and messengers sent to inform the Lords of the Council of them; and so they were committed to ward. Indeed the magistrates used them courteously, and showed them what favor they could; but could not deliver them until order came from the Council table. But the issue was, that after a month's imprisonment the greatest part were dismissed, and sent to the places from whence they came; but seven of the principal men were still kept in prison and bound over to the assizes."

In the spring of 1608 another attempt was made to embark and another Dutch shipmaster engaged. This second party assembled at a point between Grimsby and Hull not far from the mouth of the Humber. The women and children arrived in a small bark which became grounded at low water and while some of the men on shore were taken off in the ship's boat they were again apprehended. And to quote again:

"But after the first boat-full was got aboard, and she was ready to go for more, the master espied a great company, both horse and foot, with bills and guns and other weapons: for the country was raised to take them."

"But the poor men which were got on board were in great distress for their wives and children, which they saw thus to be taken, and were left distitute of their helps, and themselves also not having a cloth to shift them with, more than they had on their backs, and some scarce a penny about them, all they had being on the bark. It drew tears from their eyes, and anything they had they would have given to have been on shore again. But all in vain; there was no remedy; they must thus sadly part; and afterwards endured a fearful storm at sea, being fourteen days or more before they arrived at their port; in seven whereof they neither saw sun, moon, nor stars, and were driven to the coast of Norway; the mariners themselves often despairing of life, and once with shrieks and cries gave over all, as if the ship had been foundered in the sea, and they sinking without recovery. But when man's hope and help wholly failed, the Lord's power and mercy appeared for their recovery; for the ship rose again, and gave the mariners courage again to manager her; and if modesty would suffer me, I might declare with what fervent prayers they cried unto the Lord in this great distress, (especially some of them,) even without any great distraction."*

Those left ashore were in a pitiable state, women were left without their husbands and children without their fathers, their property had been sold in anticipation of a

*From this expression, as well as from the whole passage, there can hardly be a doubt that Bradford himself was in the vessel. The description is that of an eye witness. — Young's Chronicles, p. 29.

safe departure and the situation was, for a time at least, desperate. But a kind Providence intervened and while their purpose was thus hindered, they finally were united at Amsterdam. As Bradford states: "Notwithstanding all these storms of opposition, they all got over at length, some at one time and some at another, and yet met together again, according to their desires, with no small rejoicing."

Let us pause here a moment and reflect. In our contemplation of the present and concern for the future, we must not be unmindful of the past. It was not easy to make final decision in such matter as permanently breaking away from homes, relatives and friends, not to mention the material factors involved. Fortunately however for them and for us, this devout band was imbued with enduring faith. Faith fortified by grim determination.

Thus they planned and executed. They left the land of their nativity. They braved the perils of an unknown ocean and a still more unknown future that they might find a refuge free from religious bondage and where they might worship God according to their conscience. This they accomplished in the face of almost insurmountable hardships.

They made concord with the Indians, they builded homes, they framed laws and agreements in accordance with the time and the necessity. They established a governmental process sufficient for their needs, an outgrowth of the government of their religious life in which decisions were made by the will of the majority. They paved the way for future generations. They suffered much. They attained much. They left a heritage that must not be sacrificed.

We of today are faced with ominous problems. A rededication to the faith, vision and determination of our fathers, will be America's salvation.

## CHAPTER III Holland: An Alien Peace

They remained in Amsterdam about a year when for both material and spiritual reasons they decided to move to Leyden 22 miles distant. They had come into some contention with the church that had established itself before them which seemed difficult to settle to their satisfaction and their means of livelihood had become so restricted that they were threatened with poverty. "For these and some other reasons they removed to Leyden, a fair and beautiful city. But being now here pinched, they fell to such trades and employments as they best could, valuing peace and their spiritual comfort above any other riches whatsoever; and at length they came to raise a competent and comfortable living, but with hard and continual labor."

## The Final and Historic Decision

Some eleven or twelve years were spent in Leyden where they enjoyed "much sweet and delightful society and spiritual comfort together, in the ways of God, under the able ministry and prudent government of Mr. John Robinson and Mr. William Brewster, who was an assistant unto him in the place of an Elder, unto which he was now called and chosen by the church; so as they grew in knowledge and other gifts and graces of the spirit of God; and lived together in peace, and love, and holiness."

Yet while they seemed to have more spiritual freedom and to have enjoyed the society of their Dutch neighbors and had established a good credit among them, they were confronted with the fear of final absorption in an alien country. They preferred to maintain their language and traditions as English men and women. Moreover, King James was beginning to exercise an unwarrantable influence in the Low Countries. This went to the extreme of confiscating their types* and presses and the suppression of the religious matter printed and issued by William Brewster, the Elder of the Leyden congregation. A compelling force seemed to drive them on to seek some place of permanent settlement. And to quote from Bradford:

"Although the people generally bore all their difficulties very cheerfully and with a resolute courage, being in the best of their strength, yet old age began to come on some of them; and their great and continual labors, with other crosses and sorrows, hastened it before the time; so as it was not only probably thought, but apparently seen, that within a few years more they were in danger to scatter by necessity pressing them, or sink under their burdens, or both; and therefore, according to the divine proverb, that 'a wise man seeth the plague when it cometh, and hideth himself,' so they, like skilful and beaten soldiers, were fearful either to be entrapped or surrounded by their enemies, so as they should neither be able to fight nor

*"The printing house was searched; the type, books, and papers were seized and searched as well as sealed." — Life and Time of William Brewster. Rev. Ashbed Steele, A.M. p. 178. J. B. Lippincott and Co. 1857.

fly; and therefore thought it better to dislodge betimes to some place of better advantage and less danger, if any could be found."

"Lastly (and which was not the least,) a great hope and inward zeal they had of laying some good foundation, or at least to make way thereunto, for the propagating and advancing the Gospel of the kingdom of Christ in these remote parts of the world; yea, though they should be but as stepping-stones unto others for performing of so great a work."

"The place they had thoughts on were some of those unpeopled countries of America, which are fruitful and fit for habitation, being devoid of all civil inhabitants, where there are only savage and bruitish people, which range up and down little otherwise than the wild beasts. This proposition being made public, and coming to the scanning of all, it raised many variable opinions amongst men, and caused many fears and doubts amongst themselves. Some from their reasons and hopes conceived, labored to stir up and encourage the rest to undertake and prosecute the same; others again, out of their fears, objected against it, and sought to divert from it, alleging many things, and those neither unreasonable nor unprobable: as that it was a great design, and subject to many inconceivable perils and dangers; as, besides the casualties of the seas, (which none can be freed from,) the length of the voyage was such as the weak bodies of women and other persons worn out with age and travail, (as many of them were,) could never be able to endure; and yet if they should, the miseries of the land which they should be exposed unto would be too hard to be borne, and likely, some or all of them, to consume and utterly to ruinate them. For there they should be liable to famine, and nakedness, and the want, in the manner, of all things."

"It was answered, that all great and honorable actions were accomplished with great difficulties, and must be both enterprised and overcome with answerable courages. It was granted the dangers were great, but not desperate, and the difficulties were many, but not invincible; for although

there were many of them likely, yet they were not certain. It might be that some of the things feared might never befall them; others, by providence, care and use good of means, might in a great measure be prevented; and all of them through the help of God, by fortitude and patience, might either be borne or overcome. True it was that such attempts were not to be made and undertaken but upon good ground and reason, not rashly or lightly, as many have done for curiosity or hope of gain, etc. But their condition was not ordinary. Their ends were good and honorable, their calling lawful and urgent, and therefore they might expect a blessing of God in their proceeding; yea, although they should lose their lives in this action, yet they might have comfort in the same; and their endeavours would be honorable."*

"They lived here but as men in exile and in a poor condition; and as great miseries might possibly befall them in this place; for the twelve years of truce were now out,** and there was nothing but beating of drums and preparing for war, the events whereof are always uncertain. The Spaniard might prove as cruel as the savages of America, and the famine and pestilence are sore here and there, and their liberty less to look out for remedy."

"After many other particular things answered and alleged on both sides, it was fully concluded by the major part to put this design in execution, and to prosecute it by the best means they could."

*The age of but few is known. Carver was undoubtedly the oldest. In 1620 Elder Brewster was 56 years old, Robinson 45, Bradford 32, Edward Winslow 26, and John Howland 28.

**After the war had been raging for more than thirty years between Spain and the United Provinces, by the mediation of Henry IV of France and James I of England, a truce of twelve years was concluded on the 9th of April, 1609. This truce expired in 1621.

CHAPTER IV London: Preparation

The coast of North America was not entirely unknown. There had been several attempts at settlement and exploration. One by Sir Walter Raleigh in 1584. He had taken possession under a patent confirmed by act of Parliament, of the territory from the Carolinas north to Virginia, the name Virginia being given the new country in honor of the Virgin Queen.

In 1606 another party under command of Capt. John Smith sailed in three small vessels under authority of a charter granted by James I. They landed at a point in Chesapeake Bay, thirty-two miles from the mouth of the James river in Virginia and established a settlement called Jamestown.

In 1614 Smith made a voyage to the North Virginia coast at which time he made a comprehensive map calling this section New England. Upon his return to England he showed this map to Charles I, then a prince, who in applying the names of English towns to points along the coast gave the place which was to become the Pilgrim settlement the name of Plymouth, which it has since retained.

There were many matters of moment to be settled

before the Pilgrims could depart their native shores. The liquidation of what property they had acquired was to be augmented by further financing. It was necessary to obtain a patent to any land they might acquire for settlement and the matter of how many and who should go first had to be determined.

"Those that stayed, being the greater number, required the pastor to stay with them; and indeed for other reasons he could not then well go, and so it was the more easily yielded unto. It was also agreed on by mutual consent and convenant that those who went should be an absolute church of themselves, as well as those that stayed, seeing in such a dangerous voyage, and a removal to such a distance, it might come to pass that they should (for the body of them) never meet again in this world. Yet with this proviso, that if any of the rest came over to them, or of the other returned upon occasion, they should be reputed as members without further admission or testimonial. It was also promised to those that went first, by the body of the rest, that if the Lord gave them life and means, and opportunity, they should come to them as soon as they could."

The next step was to secure a patent. Already letters-patent had been granted two companies of Englishmen to territory 100 miles in width on the Atlantic coast of North America from the 34th to the 45th degrees north latitude. These were designated as the South and North Virginia companies. Through emissaries sent to England a patent was obtained bearing date of Feb. 12th, 1620. This patent was issued to John Pierce and Associates and covered territory in the vicinity of the Virginia Capes. As it happened the Pilgrims settled outside the limits defined therein and another patent was granted covering the territory around Cape Cod Bay. This patent bears the date of June 1st, 1621, and was issued by the Council of New England which had been created by royal authority to succeed the North Virginia Company after the departure of the Pilgrims from England.

It shows the signatures of the Duke of Lenox, the Marquis of Hamilton, the Earl of Warwick, Lord Sheffield and Sir Ferdinand Gorges. Several parts of this ancient document have broken away, including the seal of Hamilton and the seal and signature of John Pierce, the party of the second part thereto. This valuable document, the oldest state document in New England, was brought over in the Fortune in 1621 and now reposes in Pilgrim Hall.

Arrangements were concluded with a group of London business men who styled themselves the Merchant Adventurers who were in sympathy with the movement and who had agreed to finance the expedition. Perhaps they are best described by Capt. John Smith who wrote in 1624:

"The adventurers which raised the stock to begin and supply this plantation, were about seventy, some gentlemen, some merchants, some handicraftsmen, some adventuring great sums, some small, as their estates and their affection served. These dwelt most about London. They are not a corporation, but knit together by a voluntary combination in a society without constraint or penalty, aiming to do good and to plant religion."

## Articles of Agreement

The Articles of Agreement entered into with the Merchant Adventurers were as follows:—

"1. The adventurers and planters do agree, that every persons that goeth, being aged sixteen years and upward, be rated at ten pounds, and ten pounds to be accounted a single share.

2. That he that goeth in person, and furnisheth himself out with ten pounds, either in money or other provisions, be accounted as having twenty pounds in stock, and in the division shall receive a double share.

3. The persons transported and the adventurers shall continue their joint stock and partnership together the space of seven years, (except some unexpected impediments do cause the whole company to agree otherwise,) during which time all profits and benefits that are got, by trade, traffic, trucking, working, fishing, or any other means, of any person or persons, shall remain in the common stock until the division.

4. That at their coming there they choose out such a number of fit persons as may furnish their ships and boats

for fishing upon the sea; employing the rest in their several faculties upon the land, as building houses, tilling and planting the ground, and making such commodities as shall be most useful for the colony.

5. That at the end of the seven years, the capital and profits, viz., the houses, lands, goods and chattels, be equally divided among the adventurers and planters; which done, every man shall be free from other of them of any debt or detriment concerning the adventure.

6. Whosoever cometh to the colony hereafter, or putteth any into the stock, shall at the end of the seven years be allowed proportionally to the time of his so doing.

7. He that shall carry his wife and children or servants, shall be allowed for every person now aged 16 years and upward, a single share in the division; or if he provide them necessaries, a double share, or if they be between 10 years old and 16 then two of them to be reckoned for a person, both in transportation and division.

8. That such children as now go and are under the age of 10 years, have no other share in the division, but 50 acres of unmanured land.

9. That such persons as die before the seven years be expired, their executors to have their part or share at the division, proportionally to the time of their life in the colony.

10. That all such persons as are of this colony are to have their meat, drink, apparel and all provisions out of the common stock and goods of the said colony."

### False Accusations

It has been declared by some commentators that this agreement savored of communism. This interpretation is however unfair. As a matter of record it was not entirely satisfactory to the colonists but was imposed upon them by the Merchant Adventurers who, looking to the final liquidation of their advancements, preferred to hold the community as a whole to meet the obligation. Several letters written by Robert Cushman to his associates in Leyden tend to substantiate this view and emphasize that he had made the best possible terms under the circumstances.

Pertinent to the foregoing it is interesting to quote from Young's Chronicles, page 84, as follows:—"There is no foundation for this charge. The Plymouth people were not 'misguided by their religious theories,' nor influenced by an 'imitation of the primitive Christians,' in forming their joint stock company. They entered into this hard and disadvantageous engagement with the Merchant Adventurers not voluntarily, but of necessity, in order to obtain shipping for transporting themselves to America; and they put their own little property into a common fund in order to purchase provisions for the voyage. It was a partnership that was instituted, not a community of goods, as that phrase is commonly understood."

## The Embarkation

A small vessel of about sixty tons called the Speedwell and commanded by Captain Reynolds was secured in Holland and another, somewhat larger, the Mayflower, of London, commanded by Captain Jones. The Speedwell left Delft-Haven in July, 1620, with a company of thirty, including William Bradford, William Brewster, John Carver, Edward Winslow, Isaac Allerton, Samuel Fuller and John Howland. Captain Miles Standish was also a member of the company although not of the congregation. He was a soldier whose value to the Colony proved outstanding. They left with the blessing of John Robinson who intended to follow but whose dreams were never to be realized.

**Note: Dates following accord with the modern calendar except those marked O.S. indicating Old Style.**

The first party reached Southampton where the Mayflower awaited them with ninety passengers. On the fifteenth of August both vessels set sail but had gone but a short distance when the Speedwell began to leak. They put back to Dartmouth where eight days were spent in repairs when the ships again put to sea. They had covered scarcely three hundred miles when the Speedwell again began leaking. Both vessels turned back, putting into Plymouth harbor where the leaking craft was abandoned. Here eighteen of her passengers decided not to continue.

## Voyage and Arrival

The Mayflower with its added burden, now numbering one hundred and two souls, left Plymouth September 16th, 1620, and began its historic journey westward. For a goodly part of the voyage of over two months duration the ship was buffeted by equinoctial winds and high seas and, as they neared the coast, a death is recorded, that of William Butten, a youth, servant of Samuel Fuller. The records also disclose the birth of a son, Oceanus, to Stephen and Elizabeth Hopkins. "After long beating at sea they fell with that land which is called Cape Cod; the which being made and certainly known to be it, they were not a little joyful. After some deliberation had amongst themselves and with the master of the ship, they tacked about and resolved to stand for the southward (the wind and weather being fair) to find some place about Hudson River for their habitation.

"But after they had sailed the course about half the day, they fell amongst dangerous shols and roaring breakers, and they were so far entangled therewith as they conceived themselves in great danger; and the wind shrinking upon them withall; they resolved to bear up again for the Cape, and thought themselves happy to get out of those dangers before night overtook them, as by God's providence they did. And the next day they got into the Cape Harbor where they rode in safety."

It was the 21st of November (present calendar) when the Mayflower dropped anchor in the sheltered and quiet waters of Provincetown Harbor and one may well imagine the happiness and gratitude of these weary voyagers when they sighted this haven of refuge and were once more able to place their feet upon dry land. As Bradford records: "Being thus arrived in a good harbor and brought safe to land, they fell upon their knees and blessed the God of heaven who had brought them over the vast and furious ocean, and delivered them from all the perils and miseries thereof, again to set their feet on the firm and stable earth, their proper element."

On Monday the 23rd a landing was made, the men to make repairs to the shallop and the women to wash, thus establishing Monday as the generally accepted "Washday."

The Mayflower Compact was drawn up and signed in all probability before Mayflower dropped anchor in Provincetown Harbor. This document was partly the result of friction that had arisen during the voyage and the intimation that some among them might exercise their individual liberty without restraint and against the peace and welfare of the community as a whole. The text follows with Bradford's explanatory note:

"I shall a little return back and begin with a combination made by them before they came ashore, being the first foundation of their government in this place; occasioned partly by the discontented and mutinous speeches that some of the strangers amongst them had let fall from them in the ship — That when they came ashore they would use their own liberty; for none had power to command them, the patent they had being for Virginia, and not for New England, which belonged to another Government, with which the Virginia Company had nothing to do. And partly that such an act by them done (this their condition considered) might be as firm as any patent, and in some respects more sure."

## The Compact

"In the name of God, Amen. We whose names are under-written, the loyal subjects of our dread soverign Lord, King James, by the grace of God, of Great Britain, France and Ireland King, defender of the faith, etc., having under-taken, for the Glory of God, and advancement of the Christian faith, and honor of our King and country, a voyage to plant the first colony in the northern parts of Virginia, do by these presents solemnly and mutually in the presence of God, and one of another, covenant and combine ourselves together into a civil body politic, for our better ordering and preservation and furtherance of the ends aforesaid; and by virtue hereof to enact, constitute and frame such just and equal laws, ordinances, acts, constitutions and offices from time to time, as shall be thought most meet and convenient for the general good of the colony, unto which we promise all due submission and obedience. In witness whereof, we have hereunder subscribed our names at Cape Cod, the 11th of November, in the year of the reign of our sovereign lord, King James of England, France, and Ireland the eighteenth, and of Scotland the fifty-fourth. Anno Domino. 1620."

## Signers of the Compact

The earliest known list of the signers of the Compact is that contained in Morton's "New-Englands Memoriall," published in 1669. The names follow:

John Carver
William Bradford
Edward Winslow
William Brewster
Isaac Allerton
Myles Standish
John Alden
John Turner
Frances Eaton
James Chilton
John Crakston
Degory Priest
Thomas Williams
Gilbert Winslow
Edmund Margeson
Peter Brown
Richard Britterige
George Soule
Edward Tilley
John Tilley
Francis Cooke
Thomas Rogers

| | |
|---|---|
| John Billington | Thomas Tinker |
| Moses Fletcher | John Rigdale |
| John Goodman | Edward Fuller |
| Samuel Fuller | Richard Clark |
| Christopher Martin | Richard Gardiner |
| William Mullins | John Allerton |
| William White | Thomas English |
| Richard Warren | Edward Doty |
| John Howland | Edward Leister |
| Stephen Hopkins | |

"After this they chose, or rather confirmed, Mr. John Carver (a man godly and well approved amongst them) their Governor for that year."

This meeting, held in the cabin of the Mayflower, is generally accepted as the first New England town meeting, although on the 27th of February following, a meeting, later referred to, was held in the common house for the purpose of establishing a military guard at which Myles Standish was chosen captain.

On April 2nd another meeting was held on "common business" and at which laws "convenient for the common state" were passed.

From these first meetings evolved our present form of town meeting, held, and elections made, according to the will of the majority.

### Search for Permanent Settlement

On November 25th, a party of sixteen men under the leadership of Captain Standish set out on foot looking for a place for permanent settlement "having such instructions as was thought meet." They had proceeded but a short distance when they met a small party of Indians who fled upon approach. They were followed for some miles, when, darkness coming on, they made camp for the night.

The following day further exploration was made. Some Indian corn was discovered, also fresh water from which they drank being sorely in need thereof "this being the first New England water drunk of."

**Nov. 26 to 28**

Returning from the vicinity of Truro and the Pamet River to which their exploration had taken them, they saw deer and "great flocks of wild geese and ducks, but they were fearful of us."* Also signs of Indian habitation and "heaps of sand newly padled with their hands, which they, digging up, found in them divers fair Indian baskets filled with corn, and some in ears, fair and good, of divers colors, which seemed to them a goodly sight (having never seen any such before). So their time limited to them being expired, they returned to the ship, lest they should be in fear of their safety; and took with them part of the corn . . . of which on their return they were marvellously glad . . . "

The days immediately following were occupied in completing repairs to the shallop, in cutting wood and getting tools in readiness, in anticipation of a permanent landing.

With this in view a party of thirty set forth on Dec. 7, "for the better discovery of this place." They found signs of Indian habitation also "more of their corn and of their beans of various colors. The corn and beans they brought away proposing to give them good satisfaction when they should meet with any of them (as about 6 months afterward they did, to their good content)." "And here it is to be noted a special Providence of God, and a great mercy to this poor people that here they got seed to plant them corn the next year or else they might have starved, for they had none, nor any likelihood to get any until the season had been past (as the sequel did manifest)."

Not finding the desired harborage or place for permanent settlement this party returned to the Mayflower.

*It appears that at other times they were more fortunate, quote: "So we made there our rendezvous for that night under a few pine trees; and as it fell out, we got three fat geese, and six ducks to our supper, which we ate with soldiers' stomachs, for we had eaten little all that day"—Bradford's and Winslow's Journal (Young's Chronicles, p. 139).

During their absence and while the Mayflower lay in the Harbor of Provincetown, a son was born to Susanna White, wife of William White. He was named Peregrine.

## THE SHALLOP ARRIVES AT PLYMOUTH

### The Landing

On the sixteenth of December another party set out in the shallop "upon further discovery intending to circulate that deep bay of Cape Cod." This party consisted of Myles Standish, John Carver, William Bradford, Edward Winslow, John Tilley, Edward Tilley, John Howland, Richard Warren, Stephen Hopkins, Edward Dotey, John Allerton, Thomas English, the ship's mates, Mr. Clark and Mr. Coppin, and the master gunner and three sailors.

**Wed. Dec. 16**

"The weather was very cold and it froze so hard as the spray of the sea lighting on their coats, they were as if they had been glazed."

Proceeding as far as Wellfleet they discovered a party of "ten or twelve Indians very busy about a black thing,—what it was we could not tell,—until afterwards they saw us, and ran to and fro, as if they had been carrying something away. We landed a league or two from them where we made us a barricade and got firewood and set out sentinels and betook us to our lodging, such as it was." This landing was at Eastham ten miles distant.

When morning came the company was divided, eight cruising along shore in the shallop while the remainder explored the land bordering thereon. They came to the spot "where they saw the Indians the night before and found they had been cutting up a great fish like a grampus." (small whale or blackfish).

**Thurs. Dec. 17**

Nothing of importance having been discovered this day, they returned to the shallop which had come ashore at their calling. "So being weary and faint,—for we had eaten nothing all day,—we fell to make our rendezvous and get firewood and we fed upon such victuals as we had, and betook us to our rest, and we had set out our watch."

In the early morning of the 18th, they had their first encounter with the Indians "some thirty or forty of them, though some thought that they were many more." Many arrows were shot but "none of them either hit or hurt us, though many came close by us and on every side of us and some coats which hung up in our barricade were shot through and through." But after several shots were fired at them, they all left with apparently no casualties. This was the first actual encounter with the Indians.

**Fri. Dec. 18**

During the day the reunited party skirted the coast, the wind increasing during the afternoon to gale force. The boat's rudder was broken and the mast split and they were dependent upon their oars for steering. In this condition they were driven across the bay toward Saquish where the high seas prevented landing. By skillful maneuvering however they managed to round Saquish head and "although it was very dark and rained sore, yet in the end they got under the lee of a small island,* and remained there all the night in safety."

"Yet, God gave them a morning of comfort and refreshment for the next day was a fair and sunshiny day and they found themselves to be on an island secure from the Indians, where they might dry their stuff, fix their pieces and rest themselves. And this being the last day of the week, they prepared there to keep the Sabbath."

**Sat. Dec. 19**

## The Historic Landing

This Sabbath was spent on Clark's Island where they rested and held service. "On Monday they sounded the harbor and found it fit for shipping, and marched into the land,** and found divers cornfields, and little running brooks, a fit place

**Sun. Dec. 20**

*Clark's Island, probably named after Mr. Clark of the Mayflower.

**Officially recognized as Forefather's Day. The first permanent landing.

**Mon. Dec. 21** for situation; at least it was the best they could find, and the season, and their present necessity, made them glad to accept it. So they returned to their ship again with this news to the rest of their people, which did much comfort their hearts."

The romance surrounding the Rock that has become famous in history is not easily discredited. The fact is, that Elder Thomas Faunce, who was born in Plymouth in 1647 and died in 1746 at the age of ninety-nine years, made a statement a few years prior to his death, at a time when removal or covering of the rock was under contemplation, protesting vigorously at what he considered the desecration of an object of deep veneration. He stated in the presence of many hearers that his father, John Faunce, who came over in the ship Anne, had told him that it was on that rock that the Pilgrims landed as stated by them to him. It is further probable that they may have imparted this information to him directly as a number of the Mayflower passengers lived for many years subsequent to his birth.

This information has passed from generation to generation. "Plymouth Rock has now become a symbol of the Pilgrim venture into the unknown of their day and has inspired present-day Americans with a new Faith in democracy and in the American way of living."

It was during their absence on December 17th, that Dorothy Bradford, wife of William Bradford, was drowned in Provincetown harbor.

**Fri. Dec. 25** On the 25th, they set out in the Mayflower for Plymouth, but the wind being unfavorable, they failed to make the harbor and put back to Provincetown. **Sat. Dec. 26** "But it pleased God, the next day being Saturday, the wind came fair, and we put to sea again and came safely into a safe harbor." This was the first arrival of the Mayflower at Plymouth. Sunday was spent on the ship.

## A Permanent Settlement

It is evident that they were favorably impressed both with the security of the harbor and the general surroundings, although there was some division of opinion as to the best location for a permanent settlement as the following discloses: "This bay is a hopeful place, innumerable store of fowl, skate, cod, turbot and herring we have tasted of; abundance of muscles, the greatest and best that ever we saw; crabs and lobsters, in their time infinite."

"Monday we went aland manned with the master of the ship and three or four of the sailors. We marched along the coast in the woods seven or eight miles, but saw not an Indian nor an Indian house; only we found where formerly had been some inhabitants, and where they had planted their corn."

**Mon. Dec. 28**

"We found not any navigable river but four or five small running brooks of very sweet fresh water, that all ran into the sea."

They speak of the trees, the herbs and the soil, some sandy and some rich and fertile. They also speak of the streams that are beginning to fill with fish. That night they returned to the ship, "many being weary with marching."

The next day being Tuesday, Dec. 29, the party divided, some going on foot and some in the shallop. They came to a creek and "went up three English miles, a very pleasant river* at full sea. This place we had a great liking to plant in, but that it was so far from our fishing, our principal profit, and so encompassed with woods that we should be in much danger of the savages. Some of us, having a good mind for safety, to plant in the greater isle,** we crossed the bay, which is there five or six miles over. We judged it cold for our corn and some part very rocky; yet divers thought of it as a place defensible, and of great security."

**Tues. Dec. 29**

That night they returned again to the Mayflower determined to settle the next day on a permanent location.

*This was Jones River, probably named after the Mayflower's captain.
**Clark's Island where they spent their first Sabbath.

The final selection of a place for settlement is described as follows: "After our landing and viewing of the places, so well as we could, we came to a conclusion, by most voices, to set on the main land, on the first place, on a high ground, where there is a great deal of land cleared, and hath been planted with corn three or four years ago; and there is a very sweet brook, runs under the hill-side, and many delicate springs of as good water as can be drunk, and where we may harbor our shallops and boats exceeding well; and in this brook much good fish in their seasons; on the further side of the river also much corn-ground cleared. In one field is a great hill, on which we point to make a platform, and plant our ordinance, which will command all round about."

**Wed. Dec. 30**

So there we made our rendezvous, and a place for some of our people, about twenty, resolving in the morning to come all ashore and to build houses."

## CHAPTER V

## A New Home

From the foregoing the reader will readily recognize Coles Hill and Burial Hill and the site of the first fort, marked now by an appropriate tablet. Also Town Brook and the adjacent spring which has quenched the thirst of many a modern day pilgrim as well as residents of this historic town.

**1621**
**Sat.**
**Jan. 2**
**to**
**Sat.**
**Jan. 9**

During Dec. 31, and Jan. 1, a violent storm prevailed and it was Saturday, Jan. 2, before work on shore could be started. In the several days following trees were felled, timbers shaped, and work begun on the Common House and the "platform" or fort on the hill.

Allotments of land were made, first by taking notice of "how many families there were, willing all single men that had not wives, to join with some family as they thought fit, that so we might build fewer houses; which was done and we reduced them to nineteen families."

Friday and Saturday being stormy and Jan. 10 being the Sabbath, work was resumed on Monday, Jan. 11. During this period the greater number were living on the Mayflower which presumably anchored in the lower harbor, necessitated going to and fro and in bad weather seriously interferred with work on shore. It was on Monday, the 18th, that Francis Billington made a visit to the "great sea" as he thought and which he had seen from a tree the week previous. This fine pond of sparkling water "full of fish and fowl" thus derived its name Billington Sea.

**Mon Jan. 11**

**Mon. Jan. 18**

After some interruptions occasioned by bad weather, work was again resumed on the 19th. "We agreed that every man should build his own house, thinking by that course men would make more haste than working in common."

With this end in view work was resumed and "we went to labor that day in the building of our town, in two rows of houses for more safety. We divided by lot the plot of ground whereon to build our town, after the proportion formerly allotted. The common house in which for the first we made our rendezvous, being near finished, wanted only covering, it being only about twenty foot square. Some should make mortar, and some gather thatch; so that in four days half of it was thatched."

**Tues. Jan. 19 to Fri. Mar. 26**

During this period William Bradford was seriously ill which caused much concern. Two of the colony became lost in the nearby woods and after a night's exposure to cold, found their way back in an exahusted condition. Indians were seen upon several occasions. The roof of the Common House was set on fire by a spark but fortunately only the thatch burned. John Goodman was attacked by "two great wolves" but succeeded in fighting them off. A shed was built for common storage. On Sunday, Jan. 31st, they held their first meeting on land. A heavy wind on Sunday, Feb. 14th, did some damage to their houses and on Friday, Feb. 19th, the roof of the little house they had built for their sick caught fire but no serious damage re-

sulted. "That evening the master going ashore, killed five geese, which he friendly distributed among the sick people."

On Friday, Feb. 26th, a party of twelve Indians were seen near the plantation and on the same day the tools of Captain Myles Standish and Francis Cooke, who had been at work in the woods, were stolen during their absence.

On the morning of the next day, Saturday, Feb. 27th, a meeting was called, Myles Standish was chosen Captain and given authority to command in military affairs. Two Indians were seen on this day "upon the top of a hill" (Watson's Hill) but upon the approach of Captain Standish and Stephen Hopkins, they ran away.

These frequent visitations caused much alarm among the colonists and "caused us to plant our great ordinances in most convenient places."

On Saturday, Mar. 13th, they experienced their first thunderstorm. This occurred in the afternoon following a day of sunshine and warmth while "birds sang in the woods most pleasantly."

On Wednesday, Mar. 17th, though the weather was cold, it was fair and they planted their garden seed.

## Their Great Losses

Nothing has been said thus far about the crushing losses the first winter this little colony sustained through exposure and disease. Their sufferings must have been well nigh indescribable, yet history records very little complaint. William Bradford bore his sufferings with the rest and it seems fitting to quote here his vivid description:

"But that which was most sad and lamentable was, that in two or three months time half of their company died, especially in January and February, being the depth of winter, and wanting houses and other comforts, being infected with the scurvy and other diseases, which this long voyage and their inaccommodate condition had brought upon them; so as there died sometimes two or three a day, in the aforesaid time; that of 100 and odd persons, scarce 50 remained. And of these in the time of most distress, there was but 6 or 7 sound persons, who, to their great commendations be it spoken, spared no pains, night nor day, but with abundance of toil and hazard of their own health, fetched them wood, made them fires, dressed them meat, made their beds, washed their loathsome clothes, clothed and unclothed them; in a word did all the homely and necessary offices for them which dainty and queasy stomachs cannot endure to hear named; and all this willingly and cheerfully, without any grudging in the least, showing herein their true love unto their friends and brethren. A rare example and worthy to be remembered. Two of these seven were Mr. William Brewster, their reverend elder, and Myles Standish, their Captain and military commander, unto whom myself and many others, were much beholden in our low sick condition. And yet the Lord so upheld these persons, as in this general calamity they were not at all infected either with sickness or lameness. And what I have said of these, I may say of many others who died in this general visitation, and others yet living, that while they had health, yea, or any strength continuing, they were not wanting to any that had need of them. And I doubt not but their recompence is with the Lord."

They who died the first winter were buried on Coles Hill. A fitting memorial now marks the spot.

## CHAPTER VI — Samoset's Visit

On Friday, Mar. 26, an Indian walked boldly into the settlement. He saluted them in English and bade them "Welcome." He explained that his home was in Maine where he had learned some English from the captains of fishing vessels that frequented the coast in the vicinity of Monhegan Island, lying half way between the Penobscot and Kennebec Rivers and about twelve miles off the coast. From him they gathered much information. "He discoursed of the whole country and of every province and of their sagamores and their number of men and strength."

**Fri.
Mar. 26**

"He told us that the place where we now live is called 'Patuxet' and that about four years ago all the inhabitants died of an extraordinary plague and there is neither man, woman nor child remaining, as indeed we have found none; so there is none to hinder our possession, or lay claim unto it."

The night Samoset stayed at the house of Stephen Hopkins where they "watched him," being suspicious of the scattering bands previously seen. He had told them of another Indian whose name was Squanto, a native of the place who had been in England and could speak better English than himself and whom he would later bring with him.

The following day he returned to the Wampanoags whence he had come. This tribe, with the Nausets, occupied the territory lying between Narragansett Bay and Cape Cod. He also spoke particularly of the Nausets to the southeast who were one hundred strong while the former numbered approximately sixty. Massasoit was the Sachem or over-lord of the Indians in the territory stated. It appeared that the Nausets were much provoked against the English, having been deceived by a Captain Hunt who "got them under cover of trucking with them, twenty out of this very place and seven men from the Nausets, and carried them away and sold them for slaves."

**Sat. Mar. 27**

It seems that the Indian Squanto who was one of the number had fortunately made his escape and had been returned through the good offices of certain Englishmen who were friendly to the colonists.

On Sunday, March 28, Samoset again appeared, bringing with him five others. They brought with them a few skins but, it being the Sabbath, no trading was done. However, they accepted the hospitality of the settlement and "did eat liberally of our English victuals." They also returned the tools which had been taken from the woods during the absence of the settlers. That night they departed with a promise to come again. Samoset, who was reluctant to go, remained until Wednesday, May 31.

On April 1, he returned with Squanto. They reported that Massasoit, their great sagamore, with his brother Quadequina was near with all their men. "They could not express well in English what they would, but after an hour the King came to the top of a hill (Watson's Hill) over against us and had in his train sixty men, that we could well behold them, and they us. We were not willing to send our governor to them and they were unwilling to come to us."

**Thur. April 1**

Squanto was accordingly sent to confer with them and

returned with word that they should send one to "parley with him." Edward Winslow was selected to go that they might "know his mind and signify the mind and will of our governor which was to have trading and peace with him."

Hostages were exchanged and Captain Standish with a half dozen armed men met them at the brook (Town Brook) whence they were "conducted to a house then in building where we placed a green rug and three or four cushions." Here they were met by the governor and others and after due felicitations and assurances of friendship were exchanged, a treaty which may well have marked the first diplomatic agreement in New England history. It was faithfully observed by both parties during the reign of Massasoit and was in force thereafter until the breaking out of the King Philip War in 1675.

It seems of interest to state here that this outbreak was instigated by Metacom or Philip as he was called by the English. He was the youngest son of Massasoit and had succeeded his brother Wamsutta or Alexander as head of the Wampanoags. But the recital of that devastating struggle is not within the sphere of this booklet. Suffice it to say that it resulted in the practical extermination of Indians including the Narragansetts, who were hostile to the white settlers and who for some years had been a perpetual and growing menace.

### The Treaty With Massasoit

1. "That neither he nor any of his, should injure or do hurt to any of their people.

2. That if any of his did any hurt to any of theirs, he should send the offender that they might punish him.

3. That if anything were taken away from any of theirs, he should cause it to be restored; and they should do the like to his.

4. That if any did unjustly war against him, they would aid him; if any did war against them, he should aid them.

5. That he should send to his Neighbor-Confederates to certify them of this that they might not wrong them, but might be likewise comprised of these Conditions of Peace.

6. That when his men came to them upon any occasion, they should leave their bows and arrows behind them as we should do our pieces when we came to them.

Lastly, that doing thus, King James, their Sovereign Lord, would esteem him his friend and ally."

Early in April John Carver was re-elected governor and laws and regulations were made for the conduct of the colony. During this month Governor Carver died. He had come "out of the field very sick, it being a hot day; he complained greatly of his head and lay down, and within a few hours his senses failed, so as he never spoke more until he died. Whose death was much lamented, and caused great heaviness amongst them as there was cause. He was buried in the best manner they could, with some volleys of shot by all that bore arms; and his wife, being a weak woman, died within 5 or 6 weeks after him."

William Bradford was chosen governor in his stead, and not having fully recovered from his recent severe illness, wherein he had been near the point of death, Isaac Allerton was chosen to be an assistant "unto him who, by renewed election every year, continued sundry years together."

It may be stated that Bradford was re-elected to the same office no less than 30 times, for a total term of 33 years—every year from 1622* He was Governor of Plimoth Colony continuously from 1627-1656 inclusive excepting for five years when he "by importunity gat off."

On April 15th, the Mayflower left on her return voyage to England. During this month the first offence is recorded, that of John Billington who had defied the authority of Captain Standish. It seems however that the offence was more a matter of words or "opprobrious speeches" than of deeds.

*An apparent error in this count is due to the fact that in two years, or 1646 and 1649, no election was held; the governor simply carried on.

### The First Marriage

The first marriage in the colony took place on the 22nd of May, that of Edward Winslow to Susanna White, widow of William White. This marriage was performed "according to the laudable custom of the Low Countries in which they had lived, was thought most requisite to be performed by the magistrate, as being a civil thing, upon which many questions about inheritances do depend, with other things most proper to their cognizance and most consonant to the scriptures (Ruth 4) and nowhere found in the gospel to be laid on the ministers as a part of their office."

**May 22**

### The First Duel

What is recorded as the first duel fought in New England was between Edward Dotey and Edward Leister, servants of Mr. Hopkins. They fought with sword and dagger and both were wounded, one in the hand and the other in the thigh. This was the second offence for which punishment was invoked by the entire company. It was ordered that their heads and feet be tied together and to so lie for twenty-four hours. Their sufferings being great however they were released by the governor "upon their promise of better carriage."

**June 28**

### Winslow and Hopkins Visit Massasoit

The months of July and August were featured by several events of interest. On July 12, Edward Winslow and Stephen Hopkins paid a visit to Massasoit taking with them clothing and other small gifts which the chieftain gladly accepted. They learned that the Wampanoags had been greatly reduced by the plague that had visited them prior to the coming of the colonists, "wherein thousands of them died, they not being able to bury one another; their skulls and bones were found in many places, lying still above aground, where their houses and dwellings had been, a very sad spectacle to behold."

It was learned also that the Narragansetts "lived but on the other side of that great bay and were a strong people and many in number, living compact together and had not been at all touched by this wasting plague."

During the last of July John Billington, Jr., became lost in the woods lying to the south of the settlement and was forced to subsist for several days on berries and whatever nature afforded. He came in contact with an Indian plantation below Manomet whence he was conducted to the Nausets on the Cape. Word reached Massasoit who, in turn, informed the Plymouth company as to his whereabouts. A party of ten men was despatched in the shallop by the Governor and he was located and returned to the colony apparently none the worse for the experience.

## Arrival of Hobamack

It was about this time that Hobamack, another Indian, came to live at the settlement. He was a friend of Squanto and "faithful to the English until he died." During a visit to Nemasket (Middleboro) they came into conflict with a sachem named Corbitant who was a minor sachem under Massasoit and who was held to be deceitful both to his superior and the whites. Hobamack was seized and held against his will by Corbitant but being of great strength he broke away making his escape to Plymouth. Fearing that Squanto might have been killed "it was resolved to send the Captain and 14 men well armed" to investigate and to seek retribution if harm had befallen him. They entered the house of Corbitant who at the moment was away while others in attempting to leave against the Captain's orders, were injured and were later taken to Plymouth where their injuries were treated to their apparent satisfaction. Squanto was uninjured and made his way back to the settlement. Corbitant later explained that his actions were only in the nature of threats and that he intended no harm. He also sought the mediation of Massasoit to regain the friendship of the whites.

**Sept. 28**

On September 28th a party of ten men with Squanto for guide and interpreter, set out in the shallop to explore in and around Massachusetts Bay. They made friendly contact with the Indians of the neighborhood and returned with "A good quantity of beaver."

## The Fortune Arrives

On November 19th the Fortune, a vessel of small tonnage, arrived bringing Robert Cushman and thirty-five others. They brought practically no provisions except some clothing but being mostly able-bodied young men the colony was thus augmented in man power of which it had been much depleted, there remaining but fifty of the original colony at this time. They came to settle permanently and were made welcome.

**Nov. 19**

## Pierce's Attempt Fails

Let us now step ahead a few months. As the patent to the lands they now occupied arrived on the Fortune, it is not irrelevant to mention here the abortive attempt of John Pierce to get control of the Plymouth colony. On April 20, 1622, Pierce obtained another patent, superseding the first, broader in scope and running to himself, his heirs, associates and assigns forever.

As an evidence of his intention let us quote from a letter from one of the English company to Governor Bradford—"in regard he, whom you and we so confidently trusted, but only to use his name for the company, should aspire to be lord over us all, and so make you and us tenants at his will and pleasure, our assurance or patent being quite void and disannuled by his means." etc. The adventurers protested in vain and it is further stated that he demanded "500 pounds which cost him but 50 pounds" for the surrender of the patent.

Whether or not this or any sum was paid there seems to be no record. However the same letter states that "with great trouble and loss we have got Mr. John Pierce to assign over the grand patent to the company, which he had taken in his own name and made quite void our former grant."

Furthermore the records of the Council for New England which appear in Palfrey's History of New England furnish the following: "Whereas there were several differences between John Pierce citizen and clothmaker of London and the Treasurer and other the associates of him the said John Pierce that were undertaken with him for the settling and advancement of the plantation at Plymouth, in the parts of New England, said differences, after the full hearing and debating thereof before us were finally concluded upon by the offer of the said John Pierce, and mutual adoption of the said Treasurer and Company then present, in behalf of themselves and the rest of said Company, that the said associates with their undertakers and servants now settled or to be settled in Plymouth aforesaid should remain and continue tenants unto the Council established for the managing of the aforesaid affairs of New England, notwithstanding a grant, bearing date the 20th of April, 1622, by said Pierce obtained without the consent of the said associates, from the said Council, contrary to a former grant to the said Pierce made in behalf of himself and his said associates dated the 1st of June, 1621."

Thus the new patent was cancelled and the patent dated June 1st, 1621, remained in force.

— Ancient Landmarks of Plymouth. Wm. T. Davis, 1883. p. 45.

## CHAPTER VII Preparations for Winter

The harvest season drawing near, attention was given to gathering their crops and to putting their houses in readiness for the approaching winter. While some were thus engaged others were employed in fishing and their store of cod, bass and other fish seems to have been plentiful, for "'every family had their portion.'" Of water-fowl, wild turkeys and venison, there seems, at this time, to have been an abundance. They had a peck of meal a week to a person, also Indian corn in like proportion of which they had planted some twenty acres with six acres of barley and peas.

### The First Thanksgiving

"Our harvest being gotten in, our governor sent four men on fowling, that so we might after a special manner, rejoice together after we had gathered the fruits of our labors. These four, in one day, killed as much fowl as, with a little help besides, served the company almost a week. At which time, amongst other recreations, we exercised our

**Nov. 1621**

arms, many of the Indians coming amongst us, and among the rest their greatest king Massasoit with some ninety men, whom for three days we entertained and feasted;* and they went out and killed five deer, which they brought to the plantation and bestowed on our governor, and upon the captain and others."

The quotations in the few preceding paragraphs are from Bradford's history, and, more especially from Winslow's letter to a friend in England. This letter was sent when the Fortune made its return voyage. It further stated that since their arrival in the new country in spite of their reduced numbers, they had succeeded in building seven dwelling-houses and four for the use of the Plantation; that they had made friends with the Indians in the immediate vicinity and that they "walked as peacefully and safely in the woods as in the highways in England."

It is presumable that this letter was inspired, at least in part by the letter from Mr. Weston which had arrived with the Fortune. Weston was one of the Adventurers who had helped to finance the Plymouth colony. His letter which follows is cold and unsympathetic and according to both Bradford and Winslow he seems to have been a man of questionable sincerity as his unsuccessful attempt to establish a rival colony at Weymouth might indicate.

Weston's letter said in part:—"That you sent no lading in the ship is wonderful, and worthily distasted. I know your weakness was the cause of it, and I believe more weakness of judgment than weakness of hands. A quarter of the time you have spent in discoursing, arguing and consulting, would have done much more. If you mean, bona fide, to perform the conditions agreed upon, do us the favor to copy them out fair, and subscribe them with the principal of your names. And likewise give us account as particularly as you can how our moneys were laid out. And consider that the life of the business depends on the lading of this ship." etc.

If Weston had been acquainted with the condition of

*This is the origin of our Thanksgiving Day. As it extended over a period of several days, it might well be termed a season of Thanksgiving.

the Plymouth colony, their great depletion and hardships the first winter (and it is reasonable to suppose that he was, upon the return of the Mayflower) his letter seems unnecessarily harsh and unjust. It was addressed to Mr. Carver, the news of whose death had not yet reached England.

Governor Bradford's letter in reply to which he added an itemized accounting, follows in part. His dignified reproof, his presentation of conditions obtaining in the colony, the extenuating circumstances, I think the reader will agree cannot reasonably be omitted from this brief chronicle.

## Bradford's Letter

"Sir: Your large letter written to Mr. Carver, and dated the 6 of July, 1621, I have received the 10 of November, wherein (after the apology made for yourself) you lay many imputations upon him and us all. Touching him, he is departed this life, and now is at rest in the Lord from all those troubles and incumbencies with which we are yet to strive. He needs not my apology; for his care and pains were so great for the common good, both ours and yours, as that therewith (it is thought) he oppressed himself and shortened his days; of whose loss we cannot sufficiently complain. At great charges in this adventure, I confess you have been, and many losses may sustain; but the loss of his and many other honest and industrious men's lives, cannot be valued at any price. Of the one, there may be hope of recovery, but the other no recompence can make good. But I will not insist in generals but come more particularly to the things themselves. You greatly blame us for keeping the ship so long in the country, and then to send her away empty. She lay 5 weeks at Cape Cod, whilst with many a weary step (after a long journey) and the endurance of many a hard brunt, we sought out in the hard winter a place of habitation. Then we went in so tedious a time to make provision to shelter us and our goods, about which labor, many of our arms and legs can tell us to this day we were not negligent. But it pleased God to visit us then, with death daily, and with so general a disease, that the living were scarce able to bury the dead; and the well not in any measure sufficient

to tend the sick. And now to be so greatly blamed, for not freighting the ship, doth indeed go near us, and much discourage us. But you say you know we will pretend weakness; and do you think we had not cause? Yes, you tell us you believe it, but it was more weakness of judgement than of hands. Our weakness herein is great we confess, therefore we will bear this check patiently amongst the rest, till God send us wiser men. But they which told you we spent so much time in discoursing and consulting, etc., their hearts can tell their tongues they lie. They cared not, so they might salve their own sores, how they wounded others. Indeed, it is our calamity that we are (beyond expectation) yoked with some ill-conditioned people, who will never do good, but corrupt and abuse others, etc."

Unfortunately the Fortune on her return was overhauled by French pirates and all her cargo of value taken. Robert Cushman, who was aboard on his return to England, later wrote "By God's providence we got well home the 17th* of February. Being robbed by the Frenchmen by the way, and carried by them into France, and were kept there 15 days and lost all that we had that was worth taking; but thanks be to God, we escaped with our lives and ship."

*O. S.

## CHAPTER VIII Indian Trouble

After the departure of the Fortune the Plymouth colony faced a serious situation. Their provisions were not sufficient to meet the demands of their suddenly increased numbers and the threat of attack hovered over their little community.

The Narragansetts were not friendly with Massasoit and they resented the intrusion of the white settlers. Their chief Canonicus by way of warning sent a bundle of arrows wrapped in snake skin to which the Governor replied by returning the skin with bullets wrapped therein, together with the admonition that if they would prefer war to peace, they "could begin when they would." They however took the precaution to strengthen their defences and the settlement was "impaled round by the beginning of March."

Captain Standish had, in the meantime, on advice of the Governor, divided his small forces into "four squadrons and every one had their quarter appointed unto which they were to repair upon any sudden alarm. And, if there should be any cry of fire, a company were appointed for a guard, with muskets, while others quenched the same, to prevent Indian treachery."

In May the Sparrow, a fishing vessel, arrived bringing seven more passengers. In July two more vessels, the Charity, and the Swan, belonging to Mr. Weston, arrived with about sixty men who were left at the Plymouth settlement. They remained their through the summer when, upon the return of one of Weston's ships from Virginia, they were transferred to Weymouth, their original destination.

**1622**

These ships had brought the information that Mr. Weston had withdrawn from the Merchant Adventurers and had acquired a patent to land in the vicinity of Massachusetts Bay, that the men sent over were destined therefore, that they were a rough lot and, according to a letter from Mr. Cushman "were no men for them." They were, however, as well provided for as the circumstances under this added burden and their strained supply of provisions would permit, until their removal to the Weymouth Colony.

After their departure and when the supply of food was well nigh exhausted, a fishing vessel came into the harbor, from which they were able to secure a small supply of provisions that helped sustain them until the next harvest. This vessel also brought report of the Indian massacre in Virginia.

It was during the succeeding weeks that the fort was built on the hill (Burial Hill).. As Bradford says, "This summer they built a fort of good timber, both strong and comely, which was of good defence, made with a flat roof and battlements on which their ordinance were mounted and where they kept constant watch, especially in time of danger. It served them also for a meeting-house and was fitted accordingly for that use. It was a great work for them in this weakness and time of wants; but the danger of the time required it, and both the continual rumors of the fears from the Indians here, especially the Narragansetts, and also the hearing of that great massacre in Virginia, made all hands willing to despatch the same."

The next harvest turned out to be a poor one owing partly to their weakened condition and to other necessary work that they were called upon to do. But again Providence came to the rescue. Another ship, the Discovery, Captain Jones (Not Captain Christopher Jones of the Mayflower) came into the harbor. She had been sent out from England to "discover all the harbors between this and Virginia and the sholes of Cape Cod and to trade along the coast where they could."

From this ship they obtained articles which they in turn were able to exchange with the Indians for corn which they sorely needed and for beaver skins to apply to their obligations to the Adventurers.

The Swan, having been left by Mr. Weston at Weymouth and the colony there being destitute of provisions, arrangement was made with the Plymouth Colony to join them in a trading expedition along the Cape. This was made under the direction of Governor Bradford who went with them, taking Squanto as guide. At Chatham Squanto was stricken with fever and died, wherein they sustained a great loss. They succeeded in getting "about 26 or 28 hogsheads of corn and beans from the Indians," after which "the Governor took a few men and went to the inland places, to get what he could, and to fetch it home at the spring, which did help them something."

The Plymouth Colony had been warned as to the type of men who composed the Weymouth Colony. As it turned out, they were constantly fomenting discord with the Indians and some even went so far as to betray the friendship of their Plymouth neighbors. They were repeatedly in want of food and other supplies although having been at first well provided.

**1623**

Bradford states: "Many sold their clothes and bed coverings; others (so base were they) became servants to the Indians and would cut them wood and fetch them water for a cap full of corn; others fell to plain stealing, both night and day from the Indians, of which they grievously complained."

About this time word came that their friend Massasoit

was gravely ill. Following the Indian custom, Edward Winslow, together with one John Hamden, with Hobomock for guide, went to his aid and through their ministrations he recovered.

From Massasoit they learned of the conspiracy among the Indians which had spread to the Cape Indians and which he had been unable to stop. This conspiracy engendered by the treatment of the Indians by the Weston colony provided that the colony should be wiped out and that the Plymouth colony being likely to seek revenge, should also be exterminated.

"He advised them therefore to prevent it, and that speedily, by taking of some of the chief of them, before it was too late, for, he assured them of the truth thereof."

Whereupon, this news reaching Plymouth, Captain Myles Standish set out with eight men for Weymouth where he "found them in miserable condition." The Indians were openly defiant and insulting. The meeting resulted in the killing of several Indians including a large brave named Pecksuot whom Captain Standish killed in hand to hand combat. Those who remained of the Weston colony thought it best to take their leave and in the Swan sailed away for the fishing grounds off the coast of Maine provisioned with corn from the scanty store remaining with Standish. Thus the Weston colony came to end.

Weston returning later, fell into the hands of the Indians who stripped him of his belongings and reduced him to such extent that he appealed to the Plymouth Colony for help. They gave him a generous supply of beaver skins which he was able to exchange for supplies from the other vessels along the coast which was "the only foundation for his future course."

## CHAPTER IX Consolidation

Again the colony was facing a shortage of food and ways and means were discussed for raising larger and better crops. This brought about a change of the policy which had been imposed upon them in the last clause of their contract with the Merchant Adventurers. It was a practical repudiation of a policy that destroyed individual initiative. It is expressed in Bradford's own words as follows:—"So they began to think how they might raise as much corn as they could and obtain a better crop than they had done. At length, after much debate of things, the Governor (with the advice of the chief amongst them) gave way that they should set corn every man for his own and in that regard, trust to themselves. And so assigned to every family a parcel of land according to a proportion of their number for that end. This had very good success, for it made all hands very industrious, so as much more corn was planted than otherwise would have been. The women now went willingly into the field, which before would allege weakness and inability; whom to have compelled, would have been thought great tyranny and oppression."

"The experience that was had in this common course and condition, tried sundry years, and that amongst godly and sober men, may well evince the vanity of that conceit of Plato and other ancients, applauded by some of later time; that the taking away of property and bringing in community into a commonwealth, would make them happy and flourishing as if they were wiser than God. For this community was found to breed much confusion and discontent and retard much employment that would have been to their benefit and comfort. For the young men that were most able and fit for labor and service did repine that they should spend their time and strength to work for other men's wives and children without any recompence. The strong had no more of victuals and clothes than he that was weak and not able to do a quarter the other could; this was thought injustice. The aged and graver men to be ranked and equalized in labor, victuals and clothes, etc., with the younger, thought it some indignity and disrespect unto them. And for men's wives to be commanded to do service for other men, as dressing their meat, washing their clothes, etc., they deemed it a kind of slavery, neither could many husbands well brook it."

In this way provision was made for their future needs, as "God in his wisdom saw another course fitter for them."

## Arrival of Anne and Little James

In the summer of 1623 two vessels arrived, the Anne and the Little James. They brought about a hundred additional members to the Plymouth Colony, some being the wives and children of those already here. The Anne the larger vessel, having been chartered by the Adventurers, returned on September 20th, laden with clapboards and beaver. "Mr. Winslow was sent over with her to inform of all things, and procure such things as were thought needful for their present condition."

During the period before the harvest, the enlarged community subsisted mainly upon fish and shell fish, the latter apparently being in abundance. The one boat was used in turn by different groups that all might share in the labor in proportion to their number. An occasional deer made a welcome addition to their larder, and, as those who had lately arrived had brought provisions sufficient to sustain themselves, they were able to carry on until the new harvest.

This was evidently an abundant one, for as Bradford describes it; "By this time harvest was come, and instead of famine, now God gave them plenty, and the face of things was changed, to the rejoicing of the hearts of many, for which they blessed God. And the effect of their particular planting was well seen, for all had, one way and other, pretty well to bring the year about, and some of the abler and more industrious had to spare, and sell to others, so as any general want or famine has not been amongst them since to this day."

The harvest under the new conditions having proved a success it was followed by an equal division of land.

**1624**

"And to every person was given only one acre of land, to them and theirs, as near the town as might be and they had no more until the seven years had expired. The reason was that they might be kept close together both for more safety and defence, and the better improvement of the general employments."

Early this year, the time of election of officers having arrived and the members of the colony having increased, it was considered advisable to provide more assistance to the Governor. "The issue was, that as before there was but one assistant, they now chose 5, giving the Governor a double voice; and afterwards they increased them to 7, which course hath continued to this day."

In the spring Edward Winslow returned from England. His mission had two objectives, viz., to acquaint the Merchant Adventurers with the exact condition of the Plymouth Colony, their progress and their needs and to obtain certain necessary supplies. He reported dissension among the English company as a result of which, one faction sent over a Mr. Lyford who with one John Oldham, who had come over in the Anne, attempted to create an unfavorable impression in their report to the Adventurers. Letters of Oldham were intercepted, and, faced with the proof of their duplicity, which they couldn't deny, they were forced to leave the colony.

A ship-carpenter arriving on the ship with Mr. Winslow, proved of great value. He had completed the building of several small craft when he was stricken with fever. Bradford says of him: "He quickly built them 2 very good and strong shallops (which after did them great service) and a great and strong lighter, and had hewn timber for 2 catches; but that was lost, for he fell into a fever and though he had the best means the place could afford, yet he died."

### The First Cattle

An important acquisition to the colony was brought over by Mr. Winslow. This consisted of three heifers and a bull, "the first beginning of any cattle of that kind in the land." Of the increment of this small herd, mention is made later.

Mr. Winslow, who had gone back to England in the fall of 1624 now returned. He brought a letter from some of their friends in the English company to the effect that the company was dissolved and that the agreement by which they were sharers and partners was no longer in effect and that ways and means should be devised whereby their advancements would be secured. This letter states: "Now we think it but reason, that all such things that there appertain to the general, be kept and preserved together and rather increased daily, than anyway be dispersed, and, after your necessities are served, you gather together such commodities as the company yields and send them over to pay debts and clear engagements here, which are not less than 1400 pounds."

Two vessels had been sent over to expedite their settlement. The larger a cargo of dried fish, but because there was threat of war with France the master "neglected (through timerousness) his order and put first into Plymouth and after into Portsmouth.'" This was much to their loss for the cargo "would have yielded them (as such fish was sold that season) 1800 pounds, which would have enriched them."

The smaller vessel, the Little James, (before mentioned) with a cargo of 700 lbs. of beaver skins, was captured by a Turkish man-of-war.

Captain Standish had left on the larger vessel with letters and instructions to arrange with the Council of

New England and those of the company "which still clave to them" for easier terms in their purchase of supplies and future transactions. They had sustained heavy losses although there were some redeeming offsets as: "after harvest this year, they sent out a boat's load of corn 40 or 50 degrees to the eastward up a river called Kenebeck (Kennebec); it being one of those two shallops which their carpenter had built them the year before. God preserved them and gave them good success for they brought home 700 lbs. of beaver besides some other furs."

In April Captain Standish returned bringing news of the death of their former pastor, John Robinson, also that of Robert Cushman who had been active in the affairs of the colony. The year thus had a cloudy beginning. They had been unsuccessful in their fishing enterprises and had turned to the intensive cultivation of corn which not only served them as a food staple but as a medium of exchange, as money they had little of.

**1626**

At a time when they were in need of equipment to carry on their work to the best advantage, they heard that a plantation at Monhegan, owned by a Plymouth (England) company, of Merchants, was to "break up and divers useful goods sold." Whereupon Governor Bradford and Mr. Winslow "took a boat and some hands and went thither." These goods they bought in part with another party. They also acquired a "parcel of goats which they distributed at home as they saw need and occasion."

They also obtained some rugs and other commodities from a French ship that had been cast away on the coast, all of which added to their material comfort.

They had been paying a high rate of interest to the English company and they "sent Mr. Allerton into England to make a composition upon as good terms as he could (unto which some way had been made the year before by Captain Standish) but yet enjoined him not to conclude absolutely until they knew the terms." They also gave him a commission to secure further supplies for the colony.

Mr. Allerton returned from England with the needed

supplies also the agreement which he had affected with the remaining members of the English company. The essence of this agreement was that upon the payment of 1800 pounds, in yearly installments of 200 pounds, the Plymouth Colony would be relieved of their obligations. While this was approved by "all the plantation and consented unto" it was actually assumed by seven or eight "in behalf of the rest."

**1627**

The second allotment of land was made in January of this year, on the basis of first, that the original allotment wherein one acre was given to every person, should stand, and, second, that this, the second division, "should consist of twenty acres to every person, and to contain five in breadth and four in length; and so accordingly to be divided by lot, to every one which was to have a share therein." There followed several provisions, one to the effect "that fowling, fishing and hunting be free."

In May a division of cattle was made. from the three cows and bull brought over in 1624 there had been a substantial increase "which arose to this proportion: a cow to six persons or shares, and two goats to the same, which were first equalized for age and goodness and then allotted for; single persons consorting with others, as they thought good and smaller families likewise; and swine though more in number, yet by the same rule."

Mr. Allerton was again sent to England with power to conclude the contract previously alluded to, with certain provisions. These provisions, while still obligating "William Bradford, Captain Myles Standish, Isaac Allerton, etc." in the performance thereof, gave them a tangible means of securing themselves. They also sent "what beaver skins they could spare to pay some of their engagements and to defray his charge." He was also authorized to "procure a patent for a fit trading place in the river of Kenebeck." He was to express further the hope that their friends in Leyden might join them, in which case "they should thankfully accept of their love and partnership herein."

Early in the spring of 1628 Mr. Allerton returned with

the report that he had effected an arrangement whereby: "William Bradford, Governor of Plymouth in N. E., in America, Isaac Allerton, Myles Standish, William Brewster and Ed. Winslow of Plymouth, aforesaid, merchants, do by these presents for us and in our names, make, substitute and appoint James Sherley, Goldsmith, and John Beachamp, Salter, citizens of London, our true and lawful agents, factors, substitutes and assignees," etc., etc.

1628

He also brought a "reasonable supply of goods for the plantation and without those great interests as before is noted." And he "had settled things in a good and hopeful way."

He had obtained a patent for a trading post at Kennebec, "but it was so ill bounded, as they were fain to renew and enlarge it the next year."

It developed that Mr. Allerton had been taking advantage of his opportunity in his visits to England, to trade on his own account thus acquiring the profit that should by right, go to the company. These transactions were first overlooked for he had been of "good and faithful service."

About this time trading was inaugurated with the Dutch of New Amsterdam who had previously approached the Plymouth colony with that end in view. It was during this period that wampum was developed, both as a commodity and as a medium of exchange.

### The Wollaston Incident

The life of the colony was broken by some disquieting incidents. From the settlements at Wollaston (now a part of Quincy) came reports of trouble. Captain Wollaston, the founder of this colony, had departed for Virginia with some of his retainers, leaving one Fitcher to govern in his place. Among those of his party left behind was a Thomas Morton who, "having more craft than honesty, persuaded them to 'thrust out Fitcher." Whereupon, "they fell to great licentiousness and Morton became lord of misrule and maintained (as it were) a school of Atheism." They erected a Maypole around which they drank and danced. They furnished firearms to the Indians and the means of moulding shot; they danced and caroused, inviting Indian women for their consorts. This went on until the more ordered among them appealed to Plymouth to "suppress Morton and his consorts before they grew to further head and strength."

Two letters of remonstrance to Morton having been received with insolence and defiance, Captain Standish was called into action and proceeded with some others to take Morton by force. This they did after a show of resistance. He had "made fast his doors, armed his consorts, set divers dishes of powder and bullets ready on the table; and, if they had not been over armed with drink, more hurt might have been done. At length, fearing that they would do some violence to the house, he and some of his crew came out, not to yield but to shoot. But they were so steeled with drink their pieces were too heavy for them and one was so drunk that he ran his nose upon the point of a sword." Morton was taken to Plymouth and later sent to England, together with a report of his conduct to the Council of New England.

**1629**

In 1629 the colony received thirty-five additional members from the Leyden Congregation. They arrived with John Endicott and his company at Salem on the ship Mayflower (not the same Mayflower that had brought the Pilgrims to Plymouth). A charter had been granted to Endicott for territory in and around Massachusetts Bay. A letter came at this time from John Sherley addressed to Governor Bradford to the effect that "Mr. Beachamp and myself, with Mr. Andrews and Mr. Hatherly, are, with your love and liking, joined partners with you." etc.

On the 13th of January of this year a patent was granted to William Bradford and Associates. This enlarged the original grant and included territory on the Kennebec river where a trading post had already been established. This patent, bearing the signature of the Earl of Warwick, was later transferred to the Colony and is now in the Registry of Deeds at Plymouth.

## The First Settled Minister

The first settled minister was Ralph Smith, a graduate of Cambridge University, England, who had come with his family to the Massachusetts Bay Colony. He arrived in Plymouth in 1629 and served as minister until 1636. He was succeeded by John Rayner, a graduate of Magdalen College, who continued his ministry until 1654.

During Mr. Smith's incumbency it is probable that services were held in both the Fort on Burial Hill and the Common House on what is now Leyden Street as the first meeting-house which faced Town Square was not built until 1637.

**1630**

In May, 1630, the colony was further augmented by the arrival of "16 or 18" more of their Leyden brethren who had come to Boston with John Winthrop and his company. These arrivals, while welcome, increased the financial burden now resting heavily upon the shoulders of those who had assumed the obligations.

## First Capital Offence

This year John Billington, the elder who had before been charged with minor offences, was tried and executed for murder. "He was arraigned by both grand and petit jury" and "found guilty of willful murder by plain and notorious evidence."

## Their Obligations Increase

Having become dissatisfied with the way the affairs of the colony were being conducted in England, Mr. Winslow was sent over to effect an accounting while Mr. Allerton was discharged.

It developed that while the indebtedness of 1800 pounds previously assumed had been reduced to 1000 pounds, subsequent transactions engaged in by Mr. Allerton had increased their obligations by 4700 pounds. While it appears that Allerton had used the opportunity he enjoyed for his personal gain, the attitude of the Plymouth Colony toward him was one of generosity as shown by the following: "It is like, though Mr. Allerton might think not to wrong the plantation in the main, yet his own gain and private ends led him aside in these things; for it came to be known, and I have it in a letter under Mr. Sherley's hand, that in the first 2 or 3 years of his employment, he had cleared up 400 pounds and put it in a brewhouse in London, at first under Mr. Shirley's name, etc."

While the colony assumed this added burden of indebtedness, their income seems to have increased likewise. "The Lord prospered their trading" and "they made yearly large returns." Cattle and corn increased in value and thus encouraged "there was no longer holding them together, but now they must of necessity, go to their great lots; they could not otherwise keep their cattle, and, having oxen grown, they must have land for plowing and tillage."

**1632**

The influx into the Massachusetts Bay colony gave impulse to this movement and to the increase in the price of cattle and products of the plantations. It resulted in the establishments of settlements where the quality of the soil encouraged cultivation. Thus the nucleus of future towns began to appear with separate places of worship, in the territory both to the north and south of Plymouth?."

## Roger Williams

Roger Williams, who had come from the Massachusetts Bay colony to Plymouth, was born in Wales and matriculated at Pembroke College, Cambridge. Historians differ somewhat as to his teachings and practice. Perhaps Bradford understood him best. Let him speak: "Mr. Roger Williams (a man godly and zealous, having many precious parts, but very unsettled in judgment) came over first to Massachusetts, but upon some discontent, left the place and came hither (where he was friendly entertained, according to their poor ability) and exercised his gifts amongst them, and after some time was admitted a member of the church: and his teaching well approved, for the benefit whereof I still bless God, and am thankful to him, even for his sharpest admonitions and reproofs, so far as they agree with truth. He this year began to fall into some strange opinions, and from opinion to practice; which caused some controversy between

**1633**

the church and him, and in the end some discontent on his part, by occasion whereof he left them something abruptly." etc.

### Winslow Elected Governor

This year Edward Winslow was elected Governor. He was re-elected in 1634-1636-1638-1644, William Bradford serving from 1621 until his death in 1657 with the exception of these five years.

Trading was now begun on the Connecticut river and a post established there.

The Colony was attacked by an epidemic which took over twenty lives, including that of Samuel Fuller, their physician and surgeon who "had been a great help and comfort to them."

**1636**

In 1636 owing to the growth of the original plantation and the establishments of separate settlements at Scituate and Duxbury, the purely democratic rule which had obtained under the Mayflower Compact, wherein matters pertaining to the interests of the colony were settled in general assembly, was superseded by a law passed providing for government by deputies representing the several towns.

**1639**

In 1639 the first legislative body brought together representatives from the towns of Sandwich, Barnstable, Yarmouth, Taunton, Scituate, Duxbury and Plymouth. This we have representative government in its formative state.

### Boundaries Established

**1640**

In 1640 the boundaries of the Plymouth and Massachusetts Bay colonies were established. In the several patents there had been some overlapping of territory. This resulted in considerable controversy. "The Court of Massachusetts appointed some to range their lines according to the bounds of their patent, and (as they went to work) they made it to take in all Scituate and I know not how much more. Again, on the other hand, according to the line of the patent of this place, it would take in Hingham and much more within their bounds."

After much discussion it was finally settled on the 9th of April and subscribed to by William Bradford and Edward Winslow for Plymouth and John Endicott and Israell Stoughton for Massachusetts Bay.

The death of William Brewster occurred early in 1643. Bradford speaks of him in endearing terms: "I am to begin this year with that which was a matter of great sadness and mourning unto them all. About the 18th of April died my dear and loving friend, Mr. William Brewster, a man who had done and suffered much for the Lord Jesus and the gospels sake and had borne his part in well and woe with this poor persecuted church above 36 years, in England, Holland and in this wilderness and done the Lord and them faithful service in his place and calling." etc.

**1643**

## New England Confederacy

Due to the plottings of the Narragansetts and what seemed to be a general Indian conspiracy against the English settlers, it was decided to form an alliance with Connecticut for mutual protection. This is recorded in the Plymouth records as of June 6th, 1643, as follows: "It is ordered and concluded by the Court that Mr. Edward Winslow and Mr. William Collyer shall have full Commission and Authority in Name of the whole Court to subscribe the Articles of Confederation (now read in the Court) with the Massachusetts, Connecticut and New Haven and to subscribe the same in name of the whole and to affix thereto the common seal of the Government." (sic.)—Plymouth records, Hazard's Historical Collection. Volume 1. p. 496.

Shortly thereafter a final liquidation of the obligations of the Plymouth Colony to their English partners and associates was effected. This was based upon Articles of Agreement made and signed on October 15th, 1641,* by "John Atwode** (Atwood), William Bradford, Edward

*o. s

Winslow, etc." — Page 452, Bradford's History of The Plymouth Plantation.

In the face of the adversities that had beset them from the beginning and from which they were never entirely free, this seems a noteworthy achievement.

In 1649 the Town of Plymouth made choice of "seven discreet men whose duty it was to act in behalf of the town in disposing of lands; to make inquiry into the state and condition of the poor, to provide for their comfortable support and to find them employment; to direct to the proper means of relief for the aged and decrepid; and to attend to the affairs of the town generally."

**1649**

The foregoing together with a law passed in 1665 extended the functions of the board, "a group which may well have been the forerunner of our present Board of Selectmen."

## Conclusion

It would be interesting to follow in detail the development of the Plymouth Colony and its gradual transition from the primitive settlement to the flourishing shire town of the county. But this is a Pilgrim story and the writer bows to the limitations of time and space.

The Pilgrims sought refuge far from their homeland. They established a separate church, but they were still subjects of the crown. They were to know little or nothing of the future developments which were to lead eventually to complete independence from the mother country.

Nevertheless they left an unparalleled example of devotion to a cause. In pursuit of religious freedom, in reverence, in the exigencies of primitive government, they sowed the seed of an ideal Americanism, that God willing, will forever endure.

*O. S

**John Atwood was a trusted friend of James Sherley and represented him in the final adjustment. Sherlev was one of the Merchant Adventurers and a friend and benefactor of the Plymouth colony.
See letters p's 449, 454, 478, Bradford's History of Plimouth Plantation" Printed Boston 1898 from the original manuscript.

## Complete Genealogical List of "Mayflower" Passengers

**Prepared and reprinted through the courtesy of George Ernest Bowman, editor of "The Mayflower Descendant"**

The 50 passengers from whom descent can be proved:

John Alden
Isaac Allerton
  wife Mary
  daughter Mary
  daughter Remember
John Billington
  wife Eleanor
  son Francis
William Bradford
William Brewster
  wife Mary
  son Love
Peter Brown
James Chilton
  wife ———
  daughter Mary
Francis Cooke
  son John
Edward Doty
Francis Eaton
  wife Sarah
  son Samuel
Edward Fuller
  wife ———
  son Samuel
Dr. Samuel Fuller
Stephen Hopkins
  2nd wife, Elizabeth
  son Gyles (by 1st wife)
  daughter Constance (by 1st wife)
John Howland
Richard More
William Mullins
  wife Alice
  daughter Priscilla
Degory Priest
Thomas Rogers
  son Joseph
Henry Sampson
George Soule
Myles Standish
John Tilley, and wife ———
  daughter Elizabeth
Richard Warren
William White
  wife Susanna
  son Resolved
  son Peregrine
Edward Winslow

The 54 passengers from whom we cannot prove descent:

Bartholomew Allerton
John Allerton
John Billington
Dorothy Bradford
  (1st wife of William)
Wrestling Brewster
Richard Britterige
William Butten
Robert Carter
John Carver
Katherine Carver
  (wife of John)
Maid servant of the Carvers
Richard Clarke
Humility Cooper
John Crakston
  son John
Edmund Margeson
Christopher Martin
  wife ———
Desire Minter
Ellen More
Jasper More
(a boy) More
Joseph Mullins
Solomon Prower
John Rigdale
  wife Alice
Rose Standish
  (1st wife of Myles)
Elias Story
Edward Thomson
Edward Tilley
  wife Ann

——— Ely
Thomas English
Moses Fletcher
Richard Gardner
John Goodman
William Holbeck
John Hooke
Damaris Hopkins
Oceanus Hopkins
John Langmore
William Latham
Edward Leister
Thomas Tinker
wife ———
son ———
William Trevore
John Turner
son ———
son ———
Roger Wilder
Thomas Williams
Elizabeth Winslow
(1st wife of Edward)
Gilbert Winslow

## Those Who Came on the "Fortune," the "Anne" and the "Little James"

### *FORTUNE*

John Adams
William Basset and
wife Elizabeth
William Beale
Edward Bumpus
Jonathan Brewster
Clement Briggs
John Cannon
William Conner
Robert Cushman
Thomas Cushman
Stephen Dean
Philip De le Noye
Thomas Flavell
and son
Widow Ford and
children William, John, Martha
Robert Hicks
William Hilton
Bennet Morgan
Thomas Morton
Austin Nicolas
William Palmer and
son William Jr.
William Pit
Thomas Prince
Moses Simonson
Hugh Statie
James Steward
William Tench
John Winslow
William Wright

### *ANNE and LITTLE JAMES*

Anthony Annable
Jane Annable
Sarah Annable
Hannah Annable
Edward Bangs and
wife Rebecca, two children
Robert Bartlett
Fear Brewster
Patience Brewster
Mary Buckett
Edward Burcher
Mrs. Burcher
Thomas Clarke
Christopher Conant
Hester Cooke and
three children
Experience Mitchell
George Morton
Patience Morton
Nathaniel Morton
John Morton
Sarah Morton
Ephraim Morton
George Morton Jr.
Thomas Morton, Jr.
Ellen Newton
John Oldham and
wife and eight associates
Frances Palmer
Christian Penn
Joshua Pratt
James Rand

**Cuthbert Cuthbertson and wife Sarah and four children**
**Anthony Dix**
**John Faunce**
**Goodwife Flavell**
**Edmund Flood**
**Bridget Fuller**
**Timothy Hatherly**
**William Heard**
**Margaret Hicks three children**
**Mrs. William Hilton**
**William Hilton, Jr. and another child**
**Edward Holeman**
**John Jenney wife Sarah and three children**
**Robert Long**
**Nicholas Snow**
**Alice Southworth**
**Robert Ratcliffe and wife and two children**
**Francis Sprague wife Ann and daughter Mary**
**Barbara Standish**
**Thomas Tilden and wife and child**
**Stephen Tracy and wife Triphors**
**Sarah Tracey**
**Ralph Wallen and wife Joyce**
**Elizabeth Warren**
**Mary Warren**
**Ann Warren**
**Sarah Warren**
**Elizabeth Warren, Jr.**
**Abigail Warren**
**Manassah Kempton**
**Mr. Perce's two servants**

**If you've enjoyed this copy of "THE PILGRIM STORY" you'll enjoy these other books in picture and story of Pilgrim Land, and old and new Cape Cod***

**"PILGRIM GUIDE BOOK"** .................................. **25¢**
Not a mere listing, but a comprehensive pocket-size Historic Plymouth Guide in picture and fact—printed on glossy paper.

**"CAPE COD YESTERYEARS"** .................................. **50¢**
11" wide x 16" deep, 22 pages with old-time whaling, Indians, farming, Cape Cod dress, sea captains, etc. Many rare woodcuts, photos and drawings.

**"CAPE COD PILGRIM A B C COLORING BOOK** .............. **69¢**
Delightful rhyme-telling Pilgrim Story Coloring Book with child appealing cover and big, easy-to-color letters and figures.

**"TALL TALES OF CAPE COD"** .................................. **$1.50**
The only book of its kind . . . a record of rollicking Cape legends passed down from generation to generation. Beautifully illustrated.

**"YOUR CAPE COD"** .................................. **$1.50**
A beautiful photographic journal of Cape homes, doorways, house interiors, churches, artisans at work. Printed on glossy paper.

**"OF PASSION AND FIDDLESTICKS"** .................................. **$2.95**
A brand spanking new story-cookbook written on Cape Cod by Castenzio Fiorenza, owner-chef of the Cranberry Goose Restaurant in historic old Yarmouth Port.

*Available at leading Plymouth and Cape Cod stores . . . or write to "Pilgrim," Box 386, Plymouth, Mass. Add 10¢ for mailing and handling. **Prices subject to change without notice!**

REST AND COMFORT OFF THE BUSY HIGHWAY

*The*

YANKEE  TRAVLER

MOTEL

3½ MILES SOUTH OF PLYMOUTH CENTER

RTE. 3A

TEL. 746-3000

Visit PLIMOTH PLANTATION

You will walk down a dusty street lined with wooden houses. You will smell wood smoke, see food cooking and watch people carrying on the daily tasks of a 17th century farming community.

**Open daily April 1 thru November 30**
**Admission $1.25 for adults and 50 cents for children**

*On Route 3A, 2 Miles South of Plymouth Rock*

Thirsty Cape Codders and their guests from PROVINCETOWN to PLYMOUTH know where they stand on FLAVOR, QUALITY and SATISFACTION!

THE COCA-COLA BOTTLING CO. OF CAPE COD, SAGAMORE, MASS.